JACK KEV(

This book is dedicated to:

Jack Kevorkian, a good friend, and mentor.

TABLE OF CONTENTS

INTRODUCTION

I want to thank you for purchasing this book. While incarcerated, I had the pleasure of meeting the controversial Dr. Jack Kevorkian during my stay at the Thumb Correctional Center. Our first few encounters were odd, but two people so diverse from different backgrounds and cultural upbringings discovered that the difference doesn't alter the similarity in human strains.

Throughout my time with Jack, I was able to explore, enhance, and elevate my overall outlook on life and death. My friendship with Jack destroyed all of racial barriers and stereotypes, totally altering my way of thinking to a point where my concepts on life and death will never be viewed in the same light. Inside you'll read things no one knew, and if they did, they dare not mention so. I hope you find this book a good read, as I'm still working on perfecting my craft.

R.J.

PART I: THE THUMB CORRECTIONAL FACILITY

CHAPTER ONE: OUR FIRST ENCOUNTER

I arrived at the Thumb Correctional Facility located in Lapeer, Michigan, May 2004. I was gracefully into my 7th year of a 7 to 15-year sentence for manslaughter. As an aspiring writer and poet, I spent many days in the library reading, writing, and perfecting my goals and desires to one day be a successful author of children's novels.

August 1, 2004, I was summoned to the prison control center to pick up a novel by Lewis Carrol, "Through The Looking Glass." As I signed for the receipt of the book, I noticed a strange elderly Caucasian man looking over my shoulder. When our eyes met, he smiled at me and said: "That's an excellent book young man, I've read it several times, and I'm sure you will enjoy it. Lewis Carrol was an excellent writer, but he never received the recognition he rightfully deserved." He then extended his hand to greet me and said: "By the way, I'm Jack Kevorkian, and I live in the Burns housing unit. I've been here for a while, and I see that you are new here. I read a great deal myself, and if you're interested in reading some good novels, I have plenty."

I returned his greeting, and we shook hands. Most men's hands are extremely rough and calloused, but not Jack's hands. My first impression of him was that of being some sort of pervert, but the name Kevorkian did not register in my mind at the time, but I'm sure I've heard it somewhere before. I was just 25 years old at the time and richly devoted to writing children's novels. While most other young prisoners my age was being fitted for extended family's within the system, I was able to distance myself from the rampant indoctrination or recruitment into dozens of prison gangs that governed Michigan prisons.

As I was leaving the control center, I looked back and saw Mr. Kevorkian receiving about eight books. As he struggled to carry them, I courteously offered him my assistance. Thanking me very softly with a sinister grin, I said to myself. "This is one strange individual!"

Once we reached the door to his housing unit, I handed him all of his novels. In making this transition, I recognized three of the novels he had received as "Frankenstein," "Plato The Trial And Death Of Socrates," and "Hounds Of The Bakerville."

Returning to my assigned housing unit, a fellow I had known from the Wayne County Jail stopped me and said: "Watch yourself, Ramon, don't hang around Kevorkian, he killed about 120 people man, he's a real killer. He left bodies all across the state, and they are still counting them." "Is that the doctor that killed all those people, I asked." He responded: 'yeah, homeboy, that's him, he showed a guy last year how to kill himself with homemade poison, and the man ended up in a coma. Don't hang around him, I'm telling you, don't hang around him!"

Perceiving his words in part as one of fear and another part exhilaration, I accepted them with a grain of salt and a shot of penicillin. Throughout the day, I pondered his words profoundly, and I was right; I did recall the man's name, and it all suddenly came back to me.

Unlike most prisoners, I did not sit around engaging in idol gossip about other prisoners; What they're in for or who they raped, murdered, or who they knew. This behavior, more often than not, led to violent encounters or was extensively used to invade another prisoner's circle. However, in reference to Jack, the discussions about him were harmless, for the media had satisfied even the most morbid curiosity about his plight of death.

We Meet Again

Two days later, as I was sitting alone on a bench reading my Lewis Carroll novel, Jack came and sat about three feet from me. When I noticed him, I just waved hello.

He responded:

"Are you enjoying the book?" He looked around as if to be looking to see if anyone else was watching, and stated to me:

"I know by now everybody has told you who I am, but you can't believe everything you hear. These men are really strange, and you are the first young man I've seen that takes an interest in the fine art of reading great novels. We have something in common young man. I have a vast collection of books if you'd like to see my list. I'll also let you borrow a few if you promise to bring them back."

"Thank you very much; I exclaimed. I don't like to borrow anything from anybody because it causes problems, plus I don't even know you, Mr."

"Well, I'm sorry young man, if I offended you. I rarely talk to anyone in here, except men who like to read great novels, which of course, are maybe one in a million." In brushing him off as I did, I intended no harm, and unseemingly felt somewhat disenchanted, as I would soon later discover.

I continued on reading and enjoying the afternoon sun when I noticed him sitting there reading and pulling one peanut out of his pocket at a time nibbling on them. Another factor that struck me as being quite odd is that it was about 80 degrees outside, and he was wearing a winter jacket. Casting my eyes around the small yard, I noticed that he was the only prisoner wearing a coat.

The afternoon yard lasted until 3 to 4 o'clock. Even without being told what time to leave the yard, many inmates instinctively knew when yard privilege was about to end. Many prisoners would start drifting one by one to the yard gate entrance. Some of the more older and paranoid prisoners would wait until the guard's announcement over the intercom before proceeding back to their assigned unit. Historically within any prison system, a large crowd was the focal point of many military-style assaults between prisoners. I was abreast of this danger zone long before entering prison by seasoned veterans while housed in the Wayne County Jail. And I avoided a crowd at all costs. When movement time came, I dragged my feet to allow the large crowd to disburse. Strolling slowly behind me, Jack seemed to follow me casually. All the guards allowed him to linger due to his celebrity status and obvious frail stature.

Being the last few off the yard, he caught up with me and handed me one of the novels he had picked up the other day and said: "Read this young man, and you'll learn about the essence relating to the trials of me. You'll discover why life and death are one in the same when faced with irreparable damage. When you're finished, just return it back to me." Not wanting to offend this seemingly physically harmless man a second time, I accepted the novel. "Plato" The Trial And Death Of Socrates "Four Dialogues." About a year earlier, another prisoner had introduced me to Greek Philosophy. Still, Greek literature didn't excite me as did Lewis Carroll, Edgar Rice Burroughs, Charles Dickens, or F. Scott Fitzgerald.

Who Is Jack

I finished reading Lewis Carroll about three days later. With nothing to do, I decided to read the novel he had given me. The cover of the book depicted a man sitting on a bed being offered what appeared to be a cup with several other men weeping at his side. The area they were in looked like a cavern or dungeon. On the floor laid chains, as if this man had just escaped bondage.

Reading chapter one, Euthyphro, I found myself becoming more and more interested in the dialogue. It seemed that Socrates had been imprisoned for an alleged seditious act. In reference to Socrates' impending death, He explains in part his noble and just ways with his friend Euthyphro. He distinguishes himself from ordinary men by using parables to state his position before the Gods. At the same time, he displays his wisdom in justifying his actions and reactions towards those of whom so accuse him.

Before proceeding any further, I now gather why jack wanted me to read this tragic saga. More or less, I believe that he was attempting to identify himself in somewhat of the same situation in a reverse cynical way.

Unlike ordinary encounters with strangers, prison encounters are different, more unique, and much more complicated and potentially dangerous for numerous reasons. For one, men are attracted to other men based upon nationality status, geographical locations, feminine characteristics, age, athleticism, wealth, education, poverty, etc. What was Jack's angle, I asked myself.

Meanwhile, engaging in some clandestine research into Jack's activities, I inquired about his character from a few men in his housing unit. This act was totally out of character for me, and I felt extremely strange doing it. I knew that the men I asked would now have something to ponder, more or less gossip about, but I had reached the point where I didn't care.

My inquiries led me to a firm and decisive evaluation of Jack. Each person I question labeled Dr. Kevorkian as a leopard. A solitude beast by nature that rarely engages with another, and when done, it was for mating purposes only. The mating process was not your usual mating as man and woman, but a meeting of the minds. In the prison society, most men characters are identified with an animal of nature like the totem of ancient times. For instance, a "rat" is a prison informant, a "peacock" is a fledgling homosexual, and a "cow" is a seasoned homosexual. A "hawk" is a nosy prisoner who's always watching someone else. A "chicken" is a cowardly prisoner always being degraded by others, and a "skunk" is a filthy prisoner that smells awful and never bathes. A "tree jumping frog" depending on its origins, is generally classified as a religious fanatic convicted of rape and so forth. A leopard is in a category of one that is respected and often left alone. For no-one actually invades his habitat, as it was measured to some degree as taboo, and all others labeled as this sort would rally up together in defense of their own species.

When wars broke out, certain species would band together by the forces of character and identity. Such as, during a full-scale riot, all the rats, hawks, skunks, chipmunks, squirrels, and weasels would band together. In nature, the rat, skunk, chipmunks, and weasels are linked biologically to one another. The cat family, in which Jack was attached to includes the lions, tigers, leopards, panthers, mountain lions, etc.

Having now been reassured that Jack was not a weird, old, foul beast, my quest now was to discover his magnetic attraction towards me.

Within two days, I'd finished off the novel he had given me. As always, he could easily be found most afternoons sitting on a bench alone by himself. On the first impression of seeing this sickly- looking fragile man, it would appear that he was completely harmless. But he was more deadly than anyone could ever imagine. Each move he made seemed to be made in sequence to his surroundings and methodically designed. Most people moved systematically while walking, but not Jack. Everything about him was neatly structured to benefit his surroundings, for he knew that every inch he took, over half the prison yard was watching him. It seemed to annoy him being continuously watched, and I would later discover that he specifically created an illusionary tactic to amass conversation among the watchers as if to entertain them, as well as himself.

His spoken words were not your typical prison kind. He spoke with great power, clarity, and authority. He rounded each verb, adverb, and noun with precision like that of a doctor, lawyer, or man of great educational profession.

Wanting to surprise him and return the novel one afternoon, I attempted to catch him off guard with his eyes buried inside a book. I approached him from his blind side using the sun to hide my shadow within the men walking past him. But I was sorely mistaken, for he had seen me long before I made my way to him. Before I could say a word, and without turning around, he stated to me: "Did you enjoy the novel young man?" "Yes," I responded, "but why did Plato seek death over life?" Dr. Jack, as I called him, replied: "Death is not as evil as one describes it to be, and its time now that we should learn to embrace it rather than scorning those who have accepted it. Suffering from mutilating diseases, incurable sickness, and monumental pain, is it not torture? Not to mention, the fortunes of greedy insurance companies amass. Plato accepted death by his own accord. It was those who sat around him that wept, just as they wept when Jesus was nailed to the cross, unaware that he knew his life had ended. Now here comes the government smite and wicked denying people the right to die. Our United States Supreme Court has been at odds over the right to live, but no one addresses the right to die. They send young men off into battle, then glorify their deaths with medals and badges. But when one consciously chooses death, it's a criminal act. Isn't that an issuance of death? But that purpose, as to what end, only to satisfy warmongering presidents whose historical pedigree is they're defending their nation. It's nothing more than a system of self-preservation. I'm simply a pawn who sought to bring a just end to the pain and suffering of those who sought that end. Socrates expressed he was no stranger to his destiny, for he believed that death was the porthole to a more superior life. Even assuming that no one has ever returned from death, its apparent to him that everyone there had no desire to return to earth."

I was in awe at how eloquently he expressed his words. His once demeanor changed rapidly from that of a charming states-man to that of a sophisticated advocate of moral choice.

Momentarily gasping for air, he visually searched me like an x-ray scanner to interpret my response. Little did he know, I had not one, even in its mildest form.

My next question to him was, why did he choose to befriend me out of all the prisoners around him? Dr. Jack explained to me: "I imagine that you may be hard of hearing young man. I thought I told you that you are the first prisoner I've seen that enjoys read-ing great novels. Now I have to repeat myself over and over again."

Starring him straight in the face, I thought to myself that he's lucky this was not the year 2000, because, despite his fragile stature, I would have knocked him to the ground for his ignorant and arrogant response. But then again, on second thought, I asked for it.

"Have a seat young man next to my favorite area." He then asked. "Let's sit awhile and see if you can impress me about Lewis Carroll's.

I, in turn, advised him that I was only familiar with two of Carroll's works, that being. "Through The Looking Glass, and Alice In Wonderland. But more fluent in the works of author F. Scott Fitzgerald and Nathaniel Hawthorne."

This statement forced him to stand to his feet and look me over as if I was a slave on an auction block. Standing in front of me, he demanded that I name some of the works of each author. In reference to Nathaniel Hawthorne, I informed him that I had read. "The Scarlet Letter, The Luck of The Seven Gables and Young Goodman Brown." Regarding F. Scott. Fitzgerald, I mentioned that I had read "This Side Of Paradise and The Diamond As Big As The Rift."

I could tell by his uncanny facial expressions that he was quite impressed with my interest in these classical writings.

Dr. Jack then asked where I was educated and what schools did I attend. Public school, no doubt growing up in the City of Detroit. He then wanted to know where my parents educated. This is why I took offense to his probing. My silence to this question, as well as my facial expressions, altered him that the light had now turned red, and if he exceeds this warning, he may become a victim of a hit and run driver. Bowing his head in submission, he apologized for being so inquisitive about my family. I didn't mind him questioning me about my personal life, but my family was out of the question. His instant liking towards me by virtue of my literati off settled his approach. In contrast, he resorted to a higher level of that of a conversation between two students of the fine arts, whether than two convicted murderers in the midst of hundreds of other violent prone and sorted psychotic minds. I appreciated his honesty, but we all had limits to which we govern our affairs.

Pulling several torn pieces from his pockets, Dr. Jack shared with me his daily schedule, which he prepared the night before he went to bed. Inside the papers, he had folded a weekly T.V. guide documenting the movies he intended to watch that week. Although he never personally owned a television set, he would sit in the prison day room in the morning watching old movies on Turner Classic Movies and American Movie Classics.

Most prisoners, serving more than ten years, often find means to purchase their own black and white television set. But not Jack, he made the housing unit T.V. his own. Although it was our only access to a color set, he made the most of it. From time to time, the T.V. room was a very hostile setting where most men argue over watching certain programs. Special sports events such as the NBA finals or NFL or World Series playoffs, the room would be standing room only. Other than that, the first man in usually controls the operation. There was no voting on what would be watched that day. Dr. Jack, in his conscious state, had set a new standard. He loved old classic movies such as "Gone With The Wind," "The Wild Bunch," "Cleopatra," "Tarzan," "The

Hunchback," and numerous others. Many prisoners begin absorbing this acquired taste and accommodated him in most instances. For one, he was a celebrity among them who fought the system tooth and nail, and many of them honored him with great respect, although he never officially accepted that respect. Then there was that chosen few that lashed out at him by calling him names such as "Mad Jack," "Jack In The Box," "Dr. Frankenstein," "Doctor Death," "The Killer Among Us," "Executer," "Phantom Of The Opera," based on movies he loved. The average prisoner entering prison more than likely had a street name before coming to prison. And if he did not, he would find one or adopt one issued to him by other prisoners for no other reason than his conduct or character.

CHAPTER TWO:
SIMPLY KEVORKIAN

The Burns Unit

J ack refused to fall prey to this age-old traditional concept and referred to be addressed as simply Kevorkian by both prisoners and staff alike. But I was given the unique privilege of calling him, "Jack."

After thirty days into our relationship, I slowly begin to unwind. Indifference to Jack, I never really had a fixed schedule for the day ahead of me. I worked part-time as a housing unit laundryman, a most disgusting job that consisted of cleaning prisoners state-issued clothing such as pants, shirts, socks, and underwear. The prison utilized a large washing machine and dryer somewhat identical to the average neighborhood laundry mat. However, I had to bag, clean, and redistribute many prisoners' blood-stained and shit stained underwear. At times, the smell left me nauseous to the point where I would feel sick and lose my appetite throughout the day.

The rules and policies governing a prisoner's job assignment meant that he worked. His failure to do so absent any sound medical reasons resulted in disciplinary actions towards that particular prisoner. I an effort to escape this foul job assignment,

I requested to be transferred to the Burns unit, which was a non-smoking unit. The timing of this decision was worse to fair because Jack was housed in that unit.

Another reason why I requested to be transferred was based upon a large number of smokers in the Essex housing unit. And even though it was illegal to smoke in the housing units, not one smoker adhered to the rules. Each morning you would see cigarette butts all over the bathroom floor, shower, day-room, and activity room.

Two days after making the request, my Assistant Resident Unit Manager notified me around 8:30 a.m. that my request had been granted. I packed all my meager belongings such as T.V. set, Walkman, radio, books, and tennis shoes and headed for the Burns unit.

Two men were assigned to a room that was around 8 feet in length and 10 feet in width. Inside the room was two bunks, and each prisoner had a desk and locker bolted to the wall with the prisoner's room number painted on it. On the wall above the desk, there was a bulletin board for prisoners to hang their family pictures or whatever they desired. My former room-mate chose to decorate his wall with semi-nude pictures torn from Sports Illustrated magazines. Inside the door of his locker, he had pornographic images torn out of a porno magazine he feverishly used to masturbate to when I was at work. And if you're wondering how I know all of this, well, he was captured one afternoon by a female officer making rounds. Although he claimed that the officer had lied on him, I beg to differ because unbeknownst to the officer, he intentionally wanted to get caught. This is an infamous ploy of most deviates sexually charged men who have no control over their sexual desires.

For many of them would use the misconduct report as a trophy treasure to display, relish, and allow other prisoners to read over and over again. It satisfied their twisted desires, having known that the particular female had seen their penis, and described portions thereof, of their sexual exploits. A young white prisoner colorfully named "Jackoff" would buy all sexual misconduct reports he could at $20.00 a crack. "Jackoff" hailed from a wealthy upper-class family where his father was a prominent businessman, and his mother a doctor. He was sentenced to 3 to 5 years for drunk driving and crashing his Porshe while drag racing one evening, causing injury to a young girl.

His real fascination was the fine art of masturbating he had acquired from a seasoned homosexual that introduced him to the forbidden pleasure of homosexuality. His collection of sexual misconduct reports was neatly bound in a red folder hidden under his bed, and protected with his life. From time to time, he would share it with a few other freaks who enjoyed such warped pleasures. Jackoff earned his name by virtue of his actions, "jacking off, i.e., masturbating." Jackoff used the shower to satisfy his twisted craving. Rumor has it; he found his greatest pleasure during the afternoon when water in the showers turned cold. The shock of the cold water intensified his desires, and sometimes prisoners in the area could hear him screeching in the shower.

One thing about Jackoff, he had the common decency not to engage his sour acts while his roommate was in the room. Although most prisoners rarely cared what their roommates do when they're alone, I was not one of them because most guards would seek punitive vengeance against prisoners who displayed lude and insidious gestures toward their female colleagues. And another well known salient point is that most of the male guards have anticipated a sexual encounter with one or more of the female guards employed there. And yes, many of the male prisons have uniquely designed sex rings, but that's another story.

Entering the Burns unit, the first person I looked for was Jack. And there he was, sitting in the T.V. room with his winter coat on munching on peanuts one at a time watching classic movies. This time around, he didn't notice my presence unloading my property off the small cart I used to carry it over.

There were two floors in each unit, one lower and one higher. The guard's station was in the middle of a triangle and positioned where they could clearly see down each corridor; My new room is on the lower floor, and Jack's room is located on the upper floor.

Successfully escaping the filthy laundry job and a sexually disturbed roommate, I was hoping to find a more adapt coexistence in a more sound humane way. Unfortunately, I lucked out and was housed with a 65-year-old man convicted of molesting his granddaughter and her friend under the pretense that he was going to baptize them in his son's bathtub. The room was awful, books were thrown all over the floor, the curd was build up in the corners of the room, and the smell was difficult to imagine. But what the hell I thought to myself, this was home, and I was going to make the best of it no matter what.

After situating my property, I headed towards the mop closet to get a broom, dustpan, and mop, and this was when I ran into Jack coming out of the T.V. room. He walked over and shook my hand and said:

"Came over to be with old Jack, uh."

"Not exactly," I replied. "I just had to get away from that damn laundry job I had told you about. That shitty job was driving me crazy."

"So, who's your roommate, and where do you lock at?" Jack asked.

"I'm in room 21 with this old man."

"Want to know what he's in for Ramon?"

"I already know, Jack."

As fate would have it, most prisoners knew what the other prisoners were serving time for. Jack never once asked or discussed another prisoner's conviction or sentence; he just sat listening. One would be surprised by what he could actually hear by just listening. Most prisoners had no fear discussing things such as murder, drug trafficking, assault, theft, or robbery of another prisoner while Jack was in the area, for many of them knew that whatever he heard or saw, he would never repeat to the prison guards. Jack hated all of them, even the ones that tried to befriend him, issuing special privileges by giving him a new fan, extra bed lined, extra clothing, and prompt medical attention when requested.

The average prisoner requesting medical attention from the guards would be given a visual inspection. If nothing appeared abnormal, they would be directed to write to prisoner services requesting medical care, a sort of mild spinoff. Jack never had that problem when he requested to see the nurse or doctor; He was immediately issued a pass over to health services. Many prisoners envied this courtesy issued to Jack. In fact, some prisoners complained about it, but nothing ever came of their complaints. Needless to say, it changed nothing because Jack had his bid whether he liked it or not.

The Following Day

The day after my arrival, Jack offered to let me read a scrapbook he had made of all the news articles he kept since his incarceration. He wasn't boasting about his notoriety; he was more concerned with things many of the authors of newspapers and magazines had written about him. Some of the author's faces were axed out by red makers in which he described them as liars. He well-respected reporters, Dan Rather, and Barbara Walters. But many local reporters, whom names I'm not going to mention, he appeared to hate them with a passion.

Out of curiosity, I asked him why did he kill all those people, and Jack responded: "I never killed anyone Ramon, I only sought to help ease the suffering and ultimate death of those who desired to seek death. People have labeled me as some sort of monster, those Catholic assholes, physicians, comics, and government officials used my well to do methods as means of enhancing their political agenda's. And that Oakland County Prosecutor was a total asshole. He wanted one of my attorney's Geoffrey Fieger more than he wanted me. It's more to it than one can even imagine Ramon."

What seemed like a simple question opened up another new side to Jack. Breaking him off in mid-sentence, I asked him to freeze this conversation until yard time because several other prisoners in the area were eavesdropping his every word. Prisoners had several unique ways of obtaining information from sources beyond their reach. Jack was not fully abreast of one particular prisoner in the area named "Bulldog." Bulldog was serving time for running illegal dog fights in Wayne County. When the Detroit Police raided his home and garage, they found 23 fully grown pit bulls that had been bred for fighting and 12 pups. Bulldog had amassed a small fortune breeding, training, fighting, and selling dogs in L.A., Dallas, Indiana, Chicago, and New York.

While out on bond, Bulldog, in a heated argument with a female companion, slapped her to the ground and spat in her face. Three days later, her boyfriend caught up with him and sliced his tongue out, for obvious reasons I might add. Being unable to speak, he enrolled in a sign language course at the State Prison of Southern Michigan, "Jackson." Bulldog also mastered the art of reading lips. Prisoners used his specialty to infiltrate the guards whispering from long distances. Being the cold hustler he is, Bulldog charged everyone for his services. On this particular day, several prisoners anted up $10.00 worth of soap, deodorant, and toothpaste to have Bulldog spy on me and Jack's conversation.

It wasn't as if we were engaging in illegal activities. However, the "Hawk" simply wanted to know the nature of our association. For one, they had not the gall or strength to approach either of us and inquire about our business. Even two of the guards on the afternoon shift was curious about our relationship. One day one of them asked Jack was I pressing him or annoying him. Jack responded: "we're just mere associates."

That afternoon Jack and I sat on his favorite bench as we've done for over the past three months. Reaching the point of comfort, I shared with him several personal things about my family and goals in life. But on this day, I refused to allow Jack to escape from answering the question, "why did he kill those people."

PART II: THE DEATH MACHINE

CHAPTER THREE: A MEANS TO AN END

Relating to the charge in which he was convicted of, Jack adamantly swore that the only reason why he touched the "Death Machine," was because it had temporarily malfunctioned. Recalling a vivid step by step scenario, this ten-second adjustment had landed him ten years in prison, a fatal mistake that almost cost him his life.

Briefing me in part as to what led him to create the "Death Machine," Jack recalled that he was inspired by the creation of Frankenstein and Boris Karloff ingenuity in building such a fashioned machine that gave life. On the reverse side, he wanted to develop a device that could take life. Being a licensed doctor, he explained that he was abreast of every drug that could induce death or other forms of unconscious states within his profession. In 1986, enlisting the aid of a German and a Pakistani doctor, Jack debated his concept of self-induced suicide. For six long, hard months, both doctors agreed that his idea was feasible from a moral and scientific point of view, but from a legal perspective, they believed that he would encounter more than he wished to indulge. Both of them backed out in part to assist him in his medical experiment.

His German counterpart gave Jack an invitation to travel to West Germany with him and discuss the issue with his German colleagues for a more in-depth analysis governing his ideas. Turning him down, Jack, holding fast to his land of free and home of the brave doctrine, didn't want the Germans to steal or have the first crack at his idea. Day after day, Jack worked relentlessly building his suicide machine. Acquiring blueprints from Vis-Vis Associate Architects, he drafted his machine over and over again. Not wanting any of the drugs used to fall under the illegal category of narcotics, he ran into a brick wall.

Completing all the fundamental features of his design, he selected Geoffrey Fieger as his legal advocate to sketch out any criminal laws that may affect his conduct. Attorney Fieger being the skilled technician that he is, hit the law books without mercy for three months closing every possible gap that was in Jack's neatly crafted plight. Having found no criminal violations within Jack's blueprint, Fieger encouraged Jack to perform his first assisted suicide in Detroit.

The First Assisted Suicide Attempt

Jack's first host, as he recalls, was an elderly gentlemen suffering from an irreversible brain tumor. Four doctors had already determined that this man was going to die and that nothing on this earth could save him. Using this man's relatives' Jack and attorney Fieger encouraged them to obtain an affidavit from all the doctors regarding his prognosis. Without hesitation, all four doctors signed a sworn affidavit indicating that the man was indeed dying. Jack's next port of call at the behest of attorney Fieger was to tape the man's testament surrounding his desire to die. During the interview, Jack educated him on how to utilize his "Death Machine" for maximum effect.

Barely able to function, the man kept hitting the wrong switch on the machine. There were only three switches available, but in order to be successful, he must turn them on in sequence. Failure to do so would offset the procedure. Jack scheduled the execution on New Years Day. The man's family supported this ideal from day one. Several of them were angry that his estate was being drained by medical bills and didn't want the inheritance to be lost. The man's daughter, a seasoned alcoholic, just wanted to see him die.

Reminiscing over his 1st attempt at death, Jack jokingly admitted that his 1st attempt was a total failure from the start. Notifying his German associate of his plans, he immediately flew in from Hamburg to witness the event. He also enlightened Jack to the fact he had three wealthy socialites in London that were willing to pay up to $10,000 cash, no questions asked for ringside seats. Seizing this opportunity to make some extra cash, Jack ran this offer over with Fieger, who had agreed, but demanded that Jack consults with his client and family first before making any decisions.

Fieger disagreed with Jack's assessment of selling ringside seats to strangers but had no objections to other doctors taking part in his historical event. Fieger believed that he was embarking upon a milestone in the field of science by clearing the way legally for Jack's operations. However, according to Jack, his wanting to allow strangers in the middle almost cost Fieger his legal career. Casting drift of Fieger's anger, Jack apologized for his overzealous haste and happiness. Fieger accepted it and reminded him that this was a mission and not just some wild expedition into the art of death.

Two days before the event, Jack received word that his host had suddenly died. Devastated, Jack blamed Fieger for wasting valuable time in continually counseling the gentlemen over and over again. Fieger's assessment in encouraging this procedure wanted it to appear that Jack was providing a service rather than prompting the man to end his own life. Despite all the legal ramifications, Jack's haste would develop into an obsession and an addiction more potent than alcohol, drugs, and sex combined.

In search of making some connection between my first encounter with Jack and what Jack had enlightened me on about Plato Trial And Death. I asked Jack if I could reread it. He immediately issued it back to me.

He stated, "You catch on very quickly, young man, you should've been a doctor." I tried desperately over and over again to have several black doctors I knew assist me and endorse my product. Still, Fieger refused to allow it because he believed that if society as a whole sees a black man or woman in the picture, that would seriously minimize his exposure.

Rereading portions of Socrates' vivid assessment of the soul, I was slowly gaining more insight as to Jack's ideology as to death, and why he counseled many both biblically and spiritually about the essences of death and the afterlife. Indeed, bringing an end to their torrid suffering played an integral role in their decision, but Jack's concept is what stimulated me most of all.

Socrates, when speaking of the soul, advised Cebes that, the soul resembles the divine and the body of the mortal. The soul is in the very likeness of the divine, in that it remains immortal, intelligible, uniformed, indissoluble, unchangeable, etc. And that after a man is dead, the body which is the visible part of man, has a visible framework, which is called a corpse. The corpse would naturally be dissolved, decomposed and dissipated. Yet the soul, which having been purified, will elevate unto another dimension.

In short, Jack loved the Greek philosophy of death as opposed to his scientific and medical studies learned while attending college. Somewhat shameful of switching lanes to that of Greek, among others, he kept those thoughts a much-guarded secret.

We had now grown to the point where we could discuss anything; no holds barred. Although I prided myself on my Afrocentric background, I found this old fragile white man schooling me far more significant than any university could have.

Time after time, I was now becoming obsessed as to why he

chose me to travel with him through this part of his life. Unaware at the time, Jack chose me for two distinct reasons. First, He was filled with rage almost to the boiling point of suicide. Secondly, Jack had many confessions that he wanted to release. Jack finally broke down into tears, took hold of my hand, and asked me to bear with him. I agreed, he then told me that he loved me as a son and wanted me to remember his words. Several times, he offered to allow me to rewrite the diary he amassed, but I refused. The reason being, I believed someone else was more worthy than I to receive that treasure.

Jack's Younger Years

Jack explained that while growing up, his father and uncle were devoted racists that hated Jewish and Black people and that he was convinced to believe that Black people were the scourge of the earth, and Jews were devils. Again, he was fortunate by virtue of his timing in sharing this bit of information with me; because the mere utterance of racial hatred inflamed me to the point, I would frequently act impulsively with violence. But since we had now bonded, I was able to accept his misgivings and listen more with reason than anger.

Heading off to college, Jack carried with him this hatred towards Blacks and Jews. Although he never openly expressed his views, they clandestinely were laying dormant in his heart until the right spark-ignited them. During the sixties range of Dr. Martin Luther King's Civil Rights march, Jack and several of his friends decided to play a prank on a Black student at the university they attended. Meeting outside the dorm, they headed to a small utility shed. Behind the door inside a canvas bag were four white gowns and hoods labeled KKK. Jack's father was not an official member of the Ku Klux Klan (KKK), but he offered moral and financial support to the group. Adorning themselves with these costumes, they crept over to where the young black man was residing. Quietly entering his room, they jumped him, tied him up, and dragged him to a waiting car, threw him in the trunk, and sped off the campus. In a small wooded area, they pulled the young man out and placed a rope around his neck and tied him to a tree so tight that he could barely breathe.

"Nigger, go home, or find yourself hung from this tree." One of his associates pulled the young man's pajama's down, exposing his penis, then lit a cigar and drove it straight into the young man's penis. Muffled by the rag jammed into his mouth, all they could hear was the moaning of agony. Cutting the rope from the tree, they ran back to the car and took off, leaving the man lying there naked.

The next day, gossip was filtering the air about klansmen infiltrating the campus, kidnapping, and castrating a black student. None of them, except the culprits themselves, were aware of the hoax. Grieving mildly over this immoral and despicable event, Jack confessed to me that this day always haunted him years later, and he regretted that he had deprived this you man's career in medicine for a sick laugh.

Anticipating his next statement, I beat him to the punch and said: "I remind you of that young man, don't I?"

Wiping tears from his eyes, he said, "yes, you do."

The odd dilemma that brings forth culturally distant men is not uncommon in prison. In fact, it's not common in society for two strangers to one day fall in love and share their most intimate feelings. Jack, on the other hand, was a man on an island along with myself, facing the hungry clutches of cannibals. The reason I say this is because he was very, very fond of the tales of Robinson Crusoe's "Journey Among Savages" in a foreign and isolated land, where he was the only man with reason, sympathy, and understanding of the greater world outside this violent, filled jungle. My adrenaline was now at its peak, and I asked him, "whatever happened to the young black man?"

Explaining in no uncertain term, Jack abreast me to the fact that he never saw the young man again. However, he heard that the young man transferred to another University and that University paid his tuition in full. He also later discovered that one of his associates was an offspring of a second-generation klansman. And that he authorized this so-called prank because he was directed by the Alabama klansman to inflict terror in the minds of Black men and women on campus, for they believed that all the black and Jewish students were communist spies infiltrating the University for Isreal and Russia. Even with this wild indoctrination of hatred, Jack found this reasoning to be far-fetched, but he confirmed the fact that his associate believed every word of it.

Days after the prank, Jack was issued a special invitation to attend a white brotherhood meeting in the cafeteria, which he gladly accepted. Shocked to see so many young men, Jack believed that he had finally found a suitable arena in which he could expand his associations. Three professors, two administrators, and several local police were there. Only one person adorned in the infamous KKK robe was there. Strikingly, this robe was not white, but all black except a red, white, and blue KKK sign on the man's breast. This orator first ten minutes of speech impressed Jack to the point that after everyone had stopped applauding, he kept right on. When the ma started requesting those in attendance to donate money, this is when Jack's whole psychological attire drifted away.

Other young men also had issues with the sudden orator lane changing from that of racial pride to that of them issuing 25% of their total earnings to finance their political agenda. One of the professors sitting at the table behind the orator tapped his robe and motioned him towards him, whispering something in his ear. Rejecting whatever words he had spoken to him, the orator lashed out.

"You boys have two choices here and now. Wither you swear allegiance to our cause of purifying the white race or go lay down with the mongrel dogs. Make your choice today, or forever hold your peace."

What was once a Solomon peaceful atmosphere, turned into a raging gathering of men. The local police yelled out: "You asshole, you didn't explain our aims in objectives, give these boys a chance to make up their own minds. You can't just ask them to give up all of their money without telling them why Charlie. I told them not to let your stupid ass talk to these boys. Damn it, I knew it."

Screaming back at the policeman, the orator yelled: "Sit your ass down, Willie, just guard the fucking door like you've been told to boy. One by One, some of the students edged towards the door. Standing in front of them, the policemen and two professors blocked their escape. Grabbing their attention by yelling at the top of his lungs, one of the professors asked for everybody to please sit down and listen for a moment. Seeing that it lacked cleat, the meeting had now fallen apart; the professor apologized for the misunderstanding of the words used by some of the people there.

Moreover, not wanting any of them to expose what they saw and heard, the professor demanded that everyone attending this gathering swear to an oath of silence before departing. Each student raised their hand and repeated article 72 of klans order of brotherhood not to share any of their doctrines or constitutions with any infidels or non-affiliates of their organization. All of them complied simply to escape.

From this day forth, Jack distanced himself from any affiliation with race mongers. Being only 25 years old at the time, I'd never really encountered anyone that had been officially associated with the Klan during the height of the evil rights movement. Much less knew of any white man familiar with their racist views and concepts. My only contact up until that point were generic and artificial clones or want to be the racist prisoners with nazi tattoos decorating their bodies. These impostors relied on ancient remnants and artifacts drawn up by older white con artist used to attract younger white kids to perfect and enhance their nefarious drug operation and personal agenda. Standing before

32

me was a real live witness to the violent hatred of thousands, if not millions, around the world known as Jews and Blacks. Yet again, for the third time in our relationship, I had to cage my rage. Not just that, Jack, but for all white people in general. I was actively into cultural enlightenment and race pride. I truly honored and loved all the great civil rights activists such as Dr. King, Medgar Evans, Malcolm-X, Fred Hampton, and dozens of others whose lives were snuffed out for no other reason than hatred. A hatred that deprived thousands of black people the moral and spiritual enlightenment they so desired.

Jack went on to say that there were rogue government agents and hundreds of state politicians clandestinely supporting the klan, both financially, morally, and legislatively. Not out of fear, but their underscored belief that Blacks and Jews will one day turn America in the city of Sodom.

Religious fever was a powerful weapon wielded by many in all cultures. Not one religious organization, whether in prison or society who did not embrace a fanatic. In public view, many of them were denounced or disavowed. But under the surface, their support reigned around the world; Jack supported this fact.

CHAPTER FOUR:
THE SHOWDOWN

Besides acting in the capacity of that man, I voluntarily used my muscle for Jack on occasions, unbeknownst to him, of course. Early one Sunday morning, Jack stationed the T.V. set to watch Sunday morning preaching (religious programs). In his mind, this was a comic review hour compatible with an ordinary citizen in society watching the Johnny Carson show. None of the prisoners, outside of myself, knew that Jack watched these programs as entertainment. Sitting there at 8:30 in the morning, winter coat on, munching on peanuts one at a time, Jack would giggle to himself as the preacher spoke of revelations issued to him from God.

Hunching his shoulders from time to time in response to the biblical passages ministered, he smiled at me, nodding his head as if he knew the preacher was lying. On this day, Jack got up to use the restroom. A new prisoner, having just arrived from quarantine, wanted to make his presence known. Walking through the narrow passage leading to the T.V. set, he turned the station to Cartoon Network. Not one prisoner said anything, seemingly this was standard protocol before Jack's arrival. Scanning every inch of this new prisoner's physical form, I sized him up inch by inch. His chest was mildly built, displaying that he was not a weightlifter. His stomach protruded awkwardly, indicating he was overweight. His head was bald with several scars around the edge, indicating he more than likely had been pistol-whipped or beaten with a hard object. Concluding my evaluation, I was satisfied that physically, I could take him. I made the second move and turned the station back where it was just as silently as he did. Looking over my shoulder to view his facial features, I knew that timing was the key ingredient now. The longer he took to respond to my complimenting insult, the greater his fear would become.

Psychological engagements such as this were predicated on timing. Time was now an edge that I did not want to lose, so I switched into gear and shouted: "The next time someone turns this station without affording the men watching that station the benefit of asking, it's going down." It was now his move, and I'm sure he sized me up, as I did him, when I got up to turn the channel. But his physical stature compared to mines was like night and day. He had caught me fresh from completing a 1000 sets of push-ups, crunches, and my chest was swollen like a thanksgiving turkey. Wearing a sleeveless muscle shirt exposing the rippling muscles underneath, the dude walked out the T.V. room looking as if he'd lost his best friend; we had uncovered a chicken. It wasn't my idea to exploit this man's weakness. In fact, I may have saved his life because if he had succeeded in dominating the T.V. room, he more than likely would have attempted to abuse his fictitious status, which would have proved very detrimental for him in the future.

Casually returning and unaware that in his absence, a real Mexican standoff had just occurred, Jack took his favorite chair and resumed watching his program. Had Jack known I had just engaged in such an encounter, he would have been furious. Many times we discussed needless and senseless violence between men, especially men in prison. In this instance, I also knew that Jack would have been furious in returning to discover that the station had been changed. My reasoning was not founded; in this instance, I wasn't defending my honor; I was simply thinking of Jack.

Even a few of my other associates had recognized my attachment to Jack. They accused me of being Jack's bodyguard, henchmen, protector, etc. Not wanting to realize that in a sense, they were correct in part, but I blocked this thought out each time it arrived.

My reputation was not one of fear; it was one of respect. I respected everyone, even the imbeciles. I always shared with men who couldn't afford certain items out of the prison store. In the morning, men who didn't have toothpaste could always get a shot from me. I even accommodated some of the mentally challenged prisoners who crawled around the yard on all fours picking up cigarette butts. I never smoked, but it pained me at times to see these men suffering, and better yet, it hurt me to see men teasing and verbally abusing them to enhance their so-called illusionary status quo. All around, I served a much-needed purpose to these men who otherwise would have resorted to theft to get their basic needs.

My Friend Jack

One hundred days into our relationship, there wasn't anything I couldn't discuss with Jack. We had reached a point where he shared with me such things as finding blood in his stool, his first childhood sweetheart, and one unfortunate homosexual affair he had in college. Out of all our conversations, I wanted to know about a rumor an associate told me when I first met Jack. It was a rumor about him advising a prisoner on how to commit suicide with homemade poison. It didn't matter to him whether it was a wild rumor or not. Nor did he question me on where I obtained such stories about him. What mattered most was honesty in our relationship, and when I asked him about it, he smiled and said: "Sure, I did aid two prisoners in finding paradise when I first came to prison." The first gentlemen assisted I met while we were receiving physical examines at health care. He asked me about liver cancer and how long can a man live with an ALT liver enzyme of 210. I told him not very long, and he shared with me that he had been given 90 days to live, and two years of pain medication was not helping him. I instantly felt compassion towards this man. He also seemed to know more about me than I did myself. We spoke for over an hour, and he told me that he was serving time for statutory rape on a prostitute he'd met years ago. For three years, he wined and dined her, even putting her up in her very own place.

Leaving her place one night, he saw a man entering abruptly. Feeling eerie about this man, he followed him to the doorway and watched as the man banged on the door. When she came to the door, she told the man to go away. Without thinking, he shoved the man to the ground and beat him unconscious. Come to find out; the man was her father coming to beg her to return home as he'd done over the past two years. Voluntarily notifying the police, he confessed to his affair and striking the man. What surprised him the most was his discovery that the girl was only eighteen years old, he had been with her since she was fifteen. Describing how developed she was, he pulled a picture out of his pocket they had taken together at a local bar. He had three years to serve, and he knew he wasn't going to make it. He even showed me a copy of a handwritten will leaving all of his life long earnings, home, and estate to her. I, myself, would have believed that she was at least twenty years old at the time, after seeing the pictures. At any rate, talking out the side of my neck, I wrote him down a list that contained dozens of medications that he could take to end his life. I never thought he would do it; I was simply trying to ease an older man's suffering.

I asked Jack what kind of medication he told him to take. Being sharp on the tongue when he wanted to be, he laughed and said: "I hope you're not thinking about taking any." We both laughed because he knew that was out of the question.

Jack issued him a list of Seroquel, Xanax, Valium, Thorazine, Benedryl, and numerous others. Most of these medications could easily be obtained in the prison yard by men who, during the medication lines, pretend to swallow them and then, later on, sell them to other drug-seeking prisoners for a very low price. The market for these drugs was vast and expanding rapidly to the point of demand, where prisoners began extorting prisoners out of their medication. Nurses handing out the medicine barely paid attention to the men receiving their medication. All a prisoner had to do was show his I.D. card, and she would hand him the medication. Desperate drug-addicted prisoners would scar up another prisoner I.D. and pretend to be that prisoner depending on the nurse that day. The guard stationed at the door was usually so scared and confused at the enormous line of men waiting and arguing over space; so that she was only concerned about her own safety. Not one, but all the correctional officers dreaded this moment. Hours before psychotic medication lines, you could feel the tension in the air as hundreds of mentally ill patients waited to get their meds. Gathering in numbers, shaking, bobbing, and drooling at the mouth, they reminded me of a cast of dancers in the Michael Jackson thriller video. Half of them rarely bathed, and the other half was too sedated to bathe.

The stench of their combined bodies in one area could be tasted twenty feet away. Most of them wore torn clothing, the state blue shirts they wore turned grey due to lack of washing, and the armpits were black as coal. During these times, your so-called regular prisoners gave them all the space they required. If you ever encountered any disputes with any of them during this time, be prepared to go to war with them all. Once they have received their meds, they were just as peaceful as lambs. Some prisoners took the weaker and good looking ones to slaughter shortly after that. A famous predator named Locks stalked then every night. He would select young white boys as his targets. As stated over and over again, timing is a critical element that determines whether a man would survive even the mildest form of exploitation.

Locks was a housing unit porter that cleaned the T.V. room, card room, and floors during prisoner's count. Whenever he saw his designated prey laid out on his bed during count from hi psychotic medication, he would pat the prisoner's roommate to leave for a few minutes. Most prisoners accommodated Locks out of fear of his gang affiliation. Whenever a prisoner would refuse his bidding, they were usually stabbed or beaten the next day, no longer than the day after.

If that prisoner were living alone, Locks would pick the lock by using crafty homemade lock pick sets; another prisoner had designed for him to enter rooms. Once inside, Locks would pin the unsuspecting prisoner to the bed, wrap a pillowcase around his head, and rape him. Being weakened by psychotropic drugs, the prisoner could not defend himself. One prisoner he raped was so confused that he reported to his psychologist and other prisoners that he had dreams of being raped. This same prisoner was the second suicide that Jack enlisted a prisoner to do.

True to my associate's word, it wasn't a rumor about Jack advising a prisoner on how to kill himself by overdosing on medication. The first man followed Jack's advice and bought as many pills as he could find, even the ones Jack omitted or never mentioned on the list. Taking the pills, he fell into a coma, and due to the rising cost of care, they pulled the plug on him. I never knew the man's name, nor do I care to it, but one thing is for sure, Jack confessed this to me.

Let Me Help You

The younger man that continually claimed to have dreams, no nightmares, but dreams of being raped shared with two other prisoners he'd met. Catching wind of this twisted ordeal, Locks returned five days later and raped the young kid again. This time around, Locks did not hide his face and traumatized the young boy into believing that he was a God and that this was a dream from heaven sharing unbridled love with him. In his mild unconscious state, the kid believed every word of it and fell hook, line, and sinker for Locks sick and dastardly game.

Night after night, Locks entered this kid's room and systematically performed the same ritual over and over again. Locks reached a point where he started forcing his penis into the kid's mouth and relentlessly doing the same to the kid. One night, he went too far, according to Jack, the kid bitt down on Locks penis, leaving him wenching in pain. Leaving the kids room engorged in blood, Locks ran to his room, trying his best to bandage his penis. Finding no way to stop the bleeding, he reported to the guards that he snagged his penis in the metal zipper of his pants, causing a cut alongside his penis.

Reviewing his wound, the nurse had him rushed to the hospital where the doctors determined that bite marks were the cause of his cuts. Being the hardcore freak that Locks was, he refused to admit to what actually occurred. On the other end, the kid thought it was only a dream. Overhearing the tragic saga of this kid, Jack intentionally listened in on every conversation regarding him. It was well known that he had attempted suicide on numerous occasions. Just looking at the scars on his arms and wrist indicated that he had mutilated himself. A circumference mark around his neck appeared to be a tattoo, but upon closer inspection, it was a ligature mark from his attempt to hang himself. The only thing that kept him alive was the anti-depressant drugs and other medications he consumed daily.

Serving a life sentence for raping and killing a seven-year-old girl, no one respected him. Everything he owned at one time or another was taken from him by other prisoners. Guards alike disliked him like a plague and, more often than not, after being aware of the abuse against him, simply turned their backs. This fact, among many, really hurt Jack. Every roommate, he had treated him like shit. Not a day went by without somebody harassing him, threatening him, or some other degrading act was committed against him. I could never imagine what I would have done if faced with that sort of situation. For openers, there was no way on God's green earth that I would ever molest anyone. It seemed that he had decided that death was his only salvation to end the suffering.

Catching him in the bathroom alone one evening, Jack had languished for days to await this moment. Using over a dozen of his former roommates Dilaudid he had stolen, Jack handed the kid the private stash that he had saved for himself. Telling the kid that the pills would end all of his sufferings and take him to a place where God would forgive him for all of his sinful ways, the boy chewed them down. Grabbing Jack by the hand, the kid thanked him and asked:

"After I die, will I see anyone in heaven that's in my dreams?"

Jack responded: "No, my son, you will never see any of them again. You'll only find pure happiness, and when you see that young girl you killed, let her and God know that you are sorry for what you have done." The kid smiled for the first time since being imprisoned, stumbled down the hallway, rested comfortably on his bed with a bible in his hand, and died of a drug overdose.

His death was not discovered until the next afternoon when a female guard conducting her rounds discovered him. She had a particular interest in all the underprivileged prisoners, such as this young kid.

Opening his room door, she instantly recognized that he was either dead or dying. She radioed for assistance and pulled out her CPR kit. She checked his pulse for any signs of life and found none. She pulled his bedsheet over his body, said a silent prayer, and reported to her shift commander that she was depressed at the moment, and could no longer hold her post. Granting her request, her shift commander allowed her to go home and return the next day. Inconspicuously across the hall looking through the long porthole on his room door, Jack captured blow by blow of the entire event.

CHAPTER FIVE:
WHY PROLONG
THE INEVITABLE

Wondering why Jack had stolen and saved all these pills, I inquired as to why he had contemplated ending his life. Sharp as ever, Jack came back:

"I'm old and sick Ramon, and there's no guarantee that I'm going to survive the next several years. I don't want to die simplistically. If my life was to end here, I don't want the State of Michigan to have the satisfaction of believing that they've won."

"Like Socrates, when death is imminent, why make it wait or why suffer, for no other reason than fear? There comes a time when the inevitable comes into play, just as there's life, there is death. Yes, I stole the pills from one of my former roommates that suffered from cancer. He was sickly, but not as sick as he pretended to be in regards to his so-called pain. They issued him Dilaudid twice a day. Some days he would be so high, he would forget where he stashed them at, so I started stashing them for him. Plus the fact I always left my mail upside down in my desk, and every time I returned to the room, I knew he had disturbed my mail because it would be in an upward position. What he was looking for is beyond me."

Ninety percent of prisoners experience intrusions of their personal items by their roommates. Seventy-five percent of all fights result from prisoners invading another prisoner's personal belongings. Setting a trap as Jack did was standard practice. Maybe not in the same fashion, but more or less similar.

"What did you seek to accomplish in your own death?" I asked.

Jack explained: "The soul is immortal, and the flesh is just a vehicle that carries it from one destination to the next. The spirit is the legacy of the soul in which a man leaves behind. My desire is for my spirit to carry the torch of what I loved, "administering death to those who so desire it." By ending my own life, everyone would know that I dedicated my life to what I've propagated around the world. Yes, they may have labeled a madman, coward, or monster, but if twenty years after my death, my spirit rises again in someone else that will continue with my life's work; Then, that would be my ultimate purpose in ending my life if that time came. Additionally, I wanted all those assholes in opposition to my dreams to kiss my ass."

Geoffrey The Great

Ever the eloquent poet, Jack knew that I could not identify myself with any of his esoteric ideology, so I changed the subject again and asked him about his attorney Geoffrey Fieger. Examining his facial features, which he relaxed around me, depicted a sour aura as it did many times in the past when I asked about Fieger.

Sharing with me his once-great love for Fieger, Jack admitted that Fieger had given in to the raging political outcry relating to his acts of death and leaving his host in the Oakland County Sheriffs parking lot. Fieger strongly disapproved of Jack's outrageous extracurricular additions to his actions. Fieger wanted each death to be morally sound, wholesome, and straight to the point. Jack, on the other hand, wanted it to be a spectacular event with his name and face in the spotlight hosting the death.

During one session, despite Fieger's advice, Jack called the Oakland County Sheriff's office moments before the scheduled death and alerted them to his whereabouts. Within five minutes, the Sheriff's office was bursting through the door as his host was injecting the lethal substance into his veins. Unable to successfully stop the precession, they arrested Jack on the spot. Hidden in the room, Jack had installed three tape recorders and two hidden cameras.

Arraigned and given a $10,000 personal bond, Jack was released the next afternoon. A preliminary examination was scheduled (14) days later.

On the day of the hearing, the arresting officer testified that he was notified via phone and told that Jack was engaging in illegal assisted suicide. Rushing to the scene, the officer testified that he knocked on the door, and Jack opened it up and let him in, and at that point, and he arrested Jack. On cross-examination, attorney Fieger asked the officer whether he'd forced his way into the home, and the officer responded, no. Jumping and interrupting the proceedings, Jack called the officer a liar, and pulled out two video cassette tapes and started waving them around at all the spectators and reporters in the courtroom. Issuing a brief recess, the judge ordered the prosecutor, arresting officer, Jack, and Fieger into his chambers at once, to review the tapes.

Angry at Jack for not informing him of this surprise, Fieger just stared at him with frustration. The video clearly showed that Jack had left the front door open without warning. It goes on to show that Jack had left the front door open without notice. It indicates that Jack asked the officer to produce a warrant, and in response, the officer called him a mad dog killer, then pushed him to the floor, placing handcuffs on him. Taking a deep breath, the judge ordered attorney Fieger and the prosecutor to have a seat and said to them:

"Fieger, you're one of the dirtiest, pathetic, sneakiest lawyers I've ever met in my 30 years of practicing law. Mr. Prosecutor, you're one of the most gullible prosecutors I've met in my thirty years. Officer Harris, and you sir, are a disgrace to every man that wears your uniform. All of you have disrespected the honor and integrity of this court, and I should throw you all in jail. All the charges against Mr. Kevorkian are dismissed, with prejudice. And you, Mr. Fieger, can run out there and seek your fame and fortune by embarrassing this court, but I assure you, sir, if you do, I'll show you something you will never forget.

Leaving through the side entrance, used only for judges, Jack and attorney Fieger departed unseen while the mass media was waiting outside. Safely outside the court building, according to Jack, Fieger was furious. Fieger claimed that Jack had tarnished his reputation and created a lifelong enemy of both the Oakland County judge an assistant prosecuting attorney. Contrary to Jacks's amusement, Fieger was highly upset because, in their minds, nothing on this earth could convince them that Fieger didn't orchestrate the entire episode.

Taking away the video from Jack, Fieger asked him were there any more surprises he should know about, and Jack replied, "no."

Not adhering to the judge's threats, which he knew was real, he still turned the video over to the media. Fieger removed himself from ever assisting him again. By far, the press had labeled them the most ingenious and colorful teams comparable to Batman and Robin.

Jack knew that Fieger was the best lawyer in the state that could handle his case mentally, morally, and legally. He needed Fieger's counsel for advice, so he promised him that he would never release any copies of the video and audio to anyone. Having been made a mockery, the assistant prosecutor sent a memo to all police and sheriff agencies authorizing them to use proper procedures from this point on before intruding any one's premises without probable cause or a warrant. A separate memo was specifically issued regarding Jack, that indicated that before entering any establishment relating to his case, every officer must use extreme precaution and thoroughly search the premises afterward for video and audio equipment.

Fieger was aware of the dominant power of the Oakland County officials, contrary to Jack's naïve assessment of their ability to retaliate from all corners of the state. From the floor of the Michigan Senate to the chambers of the Michigan Supreme Court, Oakland County had an open-door policy with them all.

After the deaths of the older man and young kid within the prison walls, Jack informed me that he swore to himself that he would never engage in another prisoner's suicide. Jack adamantly believed that the Michigan Department of Corrections was an arena that desperately needed his services. Seeing the sick, morally bankrupt, and psychologically diminished men languishing aimlessly around him, he loathed his desire to satisfy hundreds of men wishing to die to escape the madness of prison life. Jack believed that there was a thin line between physical suffering -vs.- psychological suffering, and the most prolific edge was the conditions in which men are forced to endure within this penal system.

One hundred and eighty days had now passed with Jack and Myself. And needless to say that it had been the most exhilarating 180 days of my incarceration.

Within the shadows of these days, I have now comprehended that death, in the science of Jack, was not as evil as it seemed. Especially in the context of someone who's facing imminent death compared to one being executed for a criminal act or those destined to die a long miserable death of agony, humiliation, exploitation, and suffering. Morally, there are no distinctive differences. Legally, well, that belongs in the hands that wield it. Scientifically, it's a marvel of the Twenty-First Century. Socially, its like a diamond still perfecting its beauty. Individually, one should be able to make death a choice for him/herself, no matter what the circumstances are. Personally, I'll save that thought for my next adventure.

EPILOGUE

I shall never forget my days spent with Jack, and I sincerely apologize for intentionally omitting some of the more personal adages of his life; for those points, I'll only share upon request!!

The End!!

ACKNOWLEDGMENTS

"I have to start by thanking Jack Kevorkian for allowing me to travel on his journey while imprisoned. I would also like to thank my family and friends for encouraging and supporting me by reading early drafts, giving me advice on the cover, editing, and just their overall support."

ABOUT THE AUTHOR

Ramon Jackson (The Advocate) is the founder of "Pressure The Movement," once known as Advocates For Social Change, AFSC. He's a known community activist that fights for the rights of all citizens of Detroit, Michigan. He frequently travels from state to state to educate the young and old on the importance of Politics and how it affects the community in which they live. If you want to learn more, you can follow him on Facebook (Ramone Jackson).

Here Mr. Jackson is depicted 2nd from your right in a photo after leaving a City Council meeting.

Printed in Great Britain
by Amazon